Sex:

"The Most Fun You Can Have Without Laughing"

. . . AND OTHER QUOTATIONS

GATHERED BY
WILLIAM COLE AND
LOUIS PHILLIPS

ST. MARTIN'S PRESS • NEW YORK

Production Editor: David Stanford Burr

Design by Judy Dannecker

Library of Congress Cataloging-in-Publication Data

Sex : the most fun you can have without laughing /
    [edited by] William Cole & Louis Phillips.
            p.   cm.
        "A Thomas Dunne book."
        ISBN 0-312-05152-2
        1. Sex—Humor. I. Cole, Williams,
1919-   .   II. Phillips, Louis.
    PN6231.S54S395   1990
    306.7'0207—dc20   90-37198
                                            CIP

10 9 8 7 6 5 4 3

Contents

A Brief Introduction
(Which the Reader will Most Likely Skip)

Erica Jong was not the first to think it, but she has said it the best: "Men and women, women and men. It will never work." But if it doesn't quite work, at least it gives us something to think about, to talk about, to joke about, to laugh out loud about.

Still, it is strange that all these wonderful thoughts have been uttered, but never before gathered. If the title *The Joy of Sex* had not already been used (and used and used and used), we might have called it that. There's much joy here, as well as some animadversion. Sex, after all, is sacred, and profane, and frequently funny as hell. Thus, the last part of our title—"Without Laughing"— doesn't strictly apply. There is, after all, lots of laughing in bed. And why shouldn't there be?

Speaking of the title—coming as it does from one of Woody Allen's (or was it Marshall Brickman's?) most felicitous phrases—we found, in the course of our research, two seeming precursors of the *Annie Hall* theme. In the movie *They Drive by Night,* Ann Sheridan says to George Raft, "Dancing is the most fun you can have without laughing." On the other hand, Jerry Della Femina contends, in *From Those Wonderful Folks Who*

Gave You Pearl Harbor, that "Advertising is the most fun you can have with your clothes on." Logically, the next step would be to create advertising while dancing.

Throughout our raucous romp through literatures and demi-literatures, through speak and non-speak, we have stumbled upon numerous enlightening contrasts. In 1964, Graham Green observed (perhaps correctly) that "Fame is a powerful aphrodisiac." Twelve years later, Henry Kissinger came up with an even more powerful (more precise?) definition: "Fame is the ultimate aphrodisiac." Other parallel ideas and statements can be found in this collection. Sex, after all, has been around a long time.

Still, we refuse to claim this volume as a work of scholarship. In many cases, we have no idea how the quotations drifted in. First and foremost, it is a work of fun. Shakespeare and Freud find their way in here, as do Groucho Marx and Casey Stengel. This collection is a labor of love and high spirits ("Can we get away with *that?*"); a book of laughter that hopes to provide from time to time the shock of recognition; a book for you to read in, and to read out to others. Helen Lawrenson has observed, and we quote her somewhere in the body and flesh of the text, that "Whatever else can be said about sex it cannot be called a dignified performance."

The reader will find no dignified performance here.

—William Cole
Louis Phillips

"That was the most fun I've had without laughing."

—Woody Allen complimenting Diane
Keaton in *Annie Hall,* screenplay
by Woody Allen and Marshall
Brickman

Sex: "The Most Fun You Can Have Without Laughing"

I. DESIRE AND SEDUCTION
"He hasn't got far yet . . ."

*H*ere's to you and here's to me,
And here's to the girl with the well-shaped knee.
Here's to the man with his hand on her garter;
He hasn't got far yet, but he's a damn good starter.
—ANONYMOUS

*M*ake love to every woman you meet. If you get five percent on your outlay it's a good investment.
—ARNOLD BENNETT

*D*espite his appearance, he enjoyed a considerable sexual success among suggestible college girls, whom he would approach with the honest unappealing inquiry, "Can I jump you?"
—BRENDAN GILL, ON DYLAN THOMAS
IN *HERE AT THE NEW YORKER*

I tell the women that the face is my experience and the hands are my soul—anything to get those panties down.
—CHARLES BUKOWSKI

*T*o win a woman in the first place one must please her, then undress her, and then somehow get her clothes back on her. Finally, so that she will allow you to leave her, you've got to annoy her.
—JEAN GIRAUDOUX, *AMPHITRYON 38*

*S*he is descended from a long line that her mother listened to.
—GYPSY ROSE LEE, TALKING ABOUT
A PRETENTIOUS CHORUS GIRL

*F*lirtation is merely an expression of considered desire coupled with an admission of its impracticability.
—MARYA MANNES

*E*asy it is of a cut loaf to steal a shive, we know.
—SHAKESPEARE, *TITUS ANDRONICUS*

*F*or what happened, of course, was totally to be foreseen. The great and terrible step was taken. What else could you expect from a girl so expectant? "Sex," said Frank Harris, "is the gateway to life." So I went through that gateway in an upper room in the Café Royal.

That afternoon at the end of the session I walked back to Uncle Lexys at Warrington Crescent, reflecting on my "rise." Like a corporal made sergeant.

—ENID BAGNOLD, *AUTOBIOGRAPHY*

*A*nd the crazy part of it was even if you were *clever,* even if you spent your adolescence reading John Donne and Shaw, even if you studied history or zoology or physics and hoped to spend your life pursuing some difficult and challenging career, you *still* had a mind full of all the soupy longings that every high school girl was awash in . . . . Underneath it all you longed to be annihilated by love, to be swept off your feet, to be filled up by a giant prick spouting sperm, soapsuds, silks and satins, and, of course, money.

—ERICA JONG

*H*e in a few minutes ravished the fair creature, or at least would have ravished her, if she had not, by a timely compliance, prevented him.

—HENRY FIELDING, *JONATHAN WILDE*

*F*or that same sweet sin of lechery, I would say, as the Friar said: A young man and a young woman in a green arbor in a May morning—if God do not forgive it, I would.

—SIR JOHN HARINGTON

*B*ecause her need to love and be loved is smouldering and constant as a vestal fire, the young female is more randy than the male, whose lust rises and falls according to what is on offer.

—IRMA KURTZ, *MANTALK*

A dainty young heiress of Lincoln's Inn Fields,
  Brisk, beautiful, wealthy, and witty,
To the power of love so unwillingly yields,
  That 'tis feared she'll unpeople the city.
The sparks and the beaus all languish and die;
  Yet, after the conquest of many,
One good little marksman, that aims with one eye,
  May wound her heart deeper than any.
                —CHARLES SACKVILLE, EARL OF DORSET

---

*H*AMLET: Lady, shall I lie in your lap?
OPHELIA: No, my lord.
HAMLET: I mean, my head upon your lap?
OPHELIA: Aye, my lord.
HAMLET: Do you think I mean country matters?
OPHELIA: Think nothing, my lord.
HAMLET: That's a fair thought to lie between maids'
legs.
                —SHAKESPEARE, *HAMLET*

---

*C*ourtship consists in a number of quiet attentions, not
so pointed as to alarm, nor so vague as not to be understood.
                —LAURENCE STERNE

SHORT-SHORT STORY

*O*h, John, let's not park here.
Oh, John, let's not park.
Oh, John, let's not.
Oh, John, let's.
Oh, John.
Oh!

—AMERICAN FOLKLORE

I know there are nights when I have power, when I could put on something and walk in somewhere, and if there is a man who doesn't look at me, it's because he's gay.

—KATHLEEN TURNER

---

*T*he pill came to market and changed the sexual and real-estate habits of millions; motel chains were created to serve them.

—HERBERT GOLD

---

*Y*ou must just acknowledge deep in your heart of hearts that *people are supposed to fuck.* It is our main purpose in life, all those other activities—playing the trumpet, vacuuming carpets, reading mystery novels, eating choco-

late mousse—are just ways of passing time until you can fuck again.

—CYNTHIA HEIMEL, *SEX TIPS FOR GIRLS*

*M*en are brought up to command, women to seduce.

—SALLY KEMPTON

*D*on't grab a girl the moment you get into a taxicab. At least wait until the driver puts down the flag.

—GEORGE JEAN NATHAN

*T*here is nothing like desire for preventing the thing one says from bearing any resemblance to what one has in mind.
—MARCEL PROUST, *REMEMBRANCE OF THINGS PAST*

*M*ACDUFF: What three things does drink especially provoke?
PORTER: Marry, sir, nose-painting, sleep, and urine. Lechery, sir, it provokes, and unprovokes. It provokes the desire, but it takes away the performance: therefore, much drink may be said to be an equivocator with lechery: it makes him and it mars him; it sets him on, and it takes him off; it persuades him, and disheartens him; makes him stand to and not stand to; in conclusion, equivocates him in a sleep, and giving him the lie, leaves him.

—SHAKESPEARE, *MACBETH*

*L*oss of virginity is rational increase; and there was never virgin got till virginity was first lost.
—SHAKESPEARE, *ALL'S WELL THAT ENDS WELL*

*I*s it not strange that desire should so many years outlive performance?
—SHAKESPEARE, *HENRY IV*

*I*nfidelity, that infallible rejuvenator, calms the fear of growing old. In spite of our decreasing charms we sweep young people off their feet, for young people do not understand themselves, and fortunately for us, can still be hypnotised by those who do.

—CYRIL CONNOLLY

II. PUBLIC STATEMENTS ON PRIVATE PARTS

"Down, wanton, down!"

*D*own, wanton, down! Have you no shame
That at the whisper of Love's name,
Or Beauty's, presto! up you raise
Your angry head and stand at gaze?
—ROBERT GRAVES, *DOWN, WANTON, DOWN*

RIDDLE

*S*tiff standing on the bed,
First it's white, and then it's red.
There's not a lady in the land
That would not take it in her hand.
—OLD ENGLISH RIDDLE
(ANSWER: A CARROT)

---

*O*bscenity is whatever gives a judge an erection.
—ANONYMOUS

I thought *coq au vin* was love in a lorry.
—VICTORIA WOOD, *TALENT*

---

*L*et's forget about the six feet and talk about the seven inches.
—MAE WEST, ON BEING TOLD THAT A
NEW MALE ACQUAINTANCE WAS 6′7″

*T*he penis is the only muscle man has that he cannot flex. It is also the only extremity that he cannot control . . . . But even worse, as it affects the dignity of its owner, is its seeming obedience to that inferior thing, woman. It rises at the sight, or even at the thought of a woman.

—ELIZABETH GOULD DAVIS

*I*talian men have to make sure you know they've got a penis.

—W. H. AUDEN

A man is two people, himself and his cock. A man always takes his friend to the party. Of the two, the friend is nicer, being more able to show his feelings.

—BERYL BAINBRIDGE

*I*f I had a cock for a day, I would get myself pregnant.

—GERMAINE GREER

*I*f my aunt had balls, she'd be my uncle.

—ANONYMOUS, TWENTIETH CENTURY
(RETORT TO AN UNLIKELY SUPPOSITION)

As a young man I used to have four supple members
and one stiff one. Now I have four stiff and one supple.
—HENRI, DUC D'AUMALE

The most distressing fact of growing older is that I find
my private parts shrinking.
—CECIL BEATON
(TO WHICH GRETA GARBO IS SUPPOSED TO HAVE REJOINED:
"AH, IF ONLY I COULD SAY THE SAME.")

How's your middle leg?
Come here till I straighten it out.
—JAMES JOYCE, *ULYSSES,*
WHORE SPEAKING

Never trust a man with a small cock.
—JEAN COCTEAU

The penis mightier than the sword.
—MARK TWAIN

*J*ohn Thomas says good-night to Lady Jane, a little droopingly, but with a hopeful heart.

> —D. H. LAWRENCE, CLOSING WORDS IN
> *LADY CHATTERLEY'S LOVER*

*I*s that a gun in your pocket, or are you just glad to see me?

> —MAE WEST, *SEXTETTE*

*W*hat a jolly bunch they were, and the only one who wasn't smiling was Solly, a 70-year-old taxi driver, who was staring mournfully at his prick and intoning: "We were born together. We grew up together. We got married together. Why, oh why, did you have to die before me?"

> —JEFFREY BERNARD, *LOW LIFE*

*M*an's shame is between his legs, a fool's between his cheeks.

> —MOSES IBN EZRA

KING DAVID

*D*avid with a single stone the great Goliath slew,
But when he fucked Uriah's wife he found he needed two.

> —EUGENE FIELD

*F*reud, living at a time when women were proving their heads were no different from men's, substituted the penis for the head as the organ of male superiority, an organ women could never prove they had.

—UNA STANNARD, *MRS. MAN*

*W*hen they circumcised Herbert Samuel they threw away the wrong bit.

—DAVID LLOYD GEORGE
(VISCOUNT HERBERT SAMUEL, ENGLISH POLITICIAN)

*M*an, we're all the same cats, we're all the same *schmuck*—Johnson, me, you, every *putz* has got that one chick, he's yelling like a real dum-dum: "Please *touch* it once. Touch it once, touch it once!"

—LENNY BRUCE

*A*nd lovely Lisa, where are you, Lisa?
You gave a new meaning to the leaning tow'r of Pisa.

—COLE PORTER, *KISS ME, KATE*

*T*here is only one other profession that outranks bankers as dedicated clients, and that is the stockbroker. . . . When the stocks go up, the cocks go up!

—XAVIERA HOLLANDER

*H*is *schlang* brings to mind the fire hoses along the corridors at school. *Schlang:* the word somehow captures the brutishness, the meatiness that I admire so, the sheer mindless, weighty and unselfconscious dangle of that living piece of hose through which he passes water as thick and strong as rope.

—PHILIP ROTH

*I*n good faith, 'a cares not what mischief he does, if his weapon be out: he will foin like any devil; he will spare neither man, woman nor child.

—SHAKESPEARE, *HENRY IV*

*W*hen I discovered it, I'd do it anywhere, I'd just whip it out and get on with it.

—OLIVER JAMES

I wouldn't sue anyone for saying I had a big prick. No man would. In fact I might pay them to do it.

—JOE ORTON, *WHAT THE BUTLER SAW*

I didn't pay three pounds fifty to see half a dozen acorns and a chipolata.

—NOËL COWARD
(OF THE MALE NUDE SCENES IN DAVID STOREY'S
THE CHANGING ROOM)

———————— ∙ ∙ ————————

*T*he physiology of love. The whale with his six-foot penis, in repose. The bat—*penis libre.* Animals with a bone in the penis. Hence, *a bone on* . . . "Happily," says Gourmont, "the bony structure is lost in man." Happily? Yes, happily. Think of the human race walking around with a bone on.

The kangaroo has a double penis—one for weekdays and one for holidays.

—HENRY MILLER, *TROPIC OF CANCER*

———————— ∙ ∙ ————————

*A*s tools, pricks aren't really reliable,
One minute hard, the next pliable.
—FIONA PITT-KETHLEY

———————— ∙ ∙ ————————

*W*hat's a nice place like this doing in a girl like you?
—AMERICAN CATCH PHRASE

———————— ∙ ∙ ————————

*F*or the nicely brought-up girl, there is something that is hard to reconcile with her genteel sensibilities about walking into the inner sanctum of a complete stranger, solemnly describing her symptoms and at the end of her recital hearing the stranger say, "Will you please go into the next room and take off everything except your shoes and stockings?" It wouldn't seem so bad if it weren't for that shoes and stockings clause! To my impressionable mind it has always smacked of the more erotic refinements of Berlin during its decadence.

—CORNELIA OTIS SKINNER,
ON VISITING A GYNECOLOGIST, IN *BOTTOMS UP*

I'm as confident as Cleopatra's pussy.

—BETTE MIDLER

*N*owadays, when the models open and display their sex, they still look straight into the sucker's eyes, just the way a grocer does when he assures his customer the mango is ripe.

—IRMA KURTZ, *MANTALK*

*I*f I still had a cherry, it would have been pushed back so far I could use it for a tail-light.

—NELL KIMBALL,
HER LIFE AS AN AMERICAN MADAM, 1970

*M*any women have the gut feeling that their genitals are ugly. One reason women are gratified by oral genital relations is that is a way of saying "I like your cunt. I can eat it."

—ERICA JONG, QUOTED IN *PLAYBOY*

*A*ll women think they're ugly, even pretty women. A man who understood this could fuck more women than Don Giovanni. They *all* think their cunts are ugly . . . . They all find fault with their figures . . . . Even models and actresses, even the women you think are so beautiful that they have nothing to worry about do worry all the time.

—ERICA JONG

*P*eople will insist . . . in treating the mons veneris as though it were Mt. Everest.

—ALDOUS HUXLEY, *EYELESS IN GAZA*

*P*art of the modesty about the female genitalia stems from actual distaste. The worst name anyone can be called is *cunt*. The best thing a cunt can be is small and unobtrusive: The anxiety about the bigness of the penis is only equalled by anxiety about the smallness of the

cunt. No woman wants to find out that she has a twat like a horse-collar . . . .

—GERMAINE GREER, *THE FEMALE EUNUCH*

*O*ne strand of pubic hair can be stronger than the Atlantic cable.

—GENE FOWLER

*E*veryone knows that the only reason women complain about men's behavior during number-one activity—particularly in reference to ice-coldness—is that women will never get over the fact that women, unless they are extraordinarily nimble-footed, cannot write their names in the snow.

—ROY BLOUNT, JR.

*M*adam, you have between your legs an instrument capable of giving pleasure to thousands—and all you can do is scratch it.

—SIR THOMAS BEECHAM,
TO AN UNTALENTED WOMAN CELLIST

*I*n itself [the vagina] had an erotic appearance, like the inside of a giraffe's ear or a tropical fruit not much prized by the locals.

—KINGSLEY AMIS, *JAKE'S THING*

*W*hat part of a woman is her "now?" I only ask because I hear that everybody's "kissing her now."

—ANONYMOUS

*T*he vagina is made so artificial [*affabre* is his word] that it can accommodate itself to any penis, so that it

will give way to a long one, meet a short one, widen to a thick one, constringe to a small one: so that every Man might well enough lie with any Woman, and every Woman with any Man.
—*THE ANATOMY OF HUMAN BODIES EPITOMISED*, 1682

A woman's "no" is said with one mouth only.
—FOLK SAYING

*M*y breasts aren't actresses.
—LIV ULLMAN, ON NUDITY IN THE THEATER, IN *THE NEW YORK TIMES*

*G*raze on my lips; and if those hills be dry, Stray lower, where the pleasant fountains lie.
—SHAKESPEARE, *VENUS AND ADONIS*

*S*ometimes the photographers would pose me in a low-necked nightgown and tell me to bend down and pick up the pails. They were not shooting the pails.
—JANE RUSSELL

*T*here's an extraordinary difference between a beautiful nipple and a dull one.

—NORMAN MAILER

*O*n the 100th anniversary of the *National Geographic* I recalled how as a kid I used to look at that magazine for photographs of topless natives. It was permissible to show such nakedness because these were women of color. Of course, this was before *Playboy, Penthouse,* and *Hustler,* but even these men's magazines have an unspoken agreement never to show nipples on the cover, no matter how gynecological they get on the inside pages, where sweaty ladies appear to be searching in vain for lost objects.

—PAUL KRASSNER

I'll come no more behind your scenes, David; for the silk stockings and white bosoms of your actresses stimulate my amorous propensities.

—SAMUEL JOHNSON TO DAVID GARRICK

"UPON THE NIPPLES OF JULIA'S BREAST"

*H*ave ye beheld (with much delight)
A red rose peeping through a white?
Or else a cherry (double grac'd)
Within a lily? Centre plac'd?
Or ever mark'd the pretty beam,
A strawberry shows half drown'd in cream?
Or seen rich rubies blushing through
A pure smooth pearl, and orient too?
So like this, nay all the rest,
Is each neat niplet of her breast.

—ROBERT HERRICK

*T*he degree of attention which breasts receive, combined with the confusion about what the breast fetishists actually want, makes women unduly anxious about them. They can never be just right; they must always be too small, too big, the wrong shape, too flabby. The characteristics of the mammary stereotype are impossible to emulate because they are falsely simulated, but they must be faked somehow or another. Reality is either gross or scrawny.

—GERMAINE GREER, *THE FEMALE EUNUCH*

*T*here is no sign that her acting would ever have progressed beyond the scope of the restless shoulders and the protuberant breasts; her body technique was the gangster's technique—she toted a breast like a man totes a gun.

—GRAHAM GREENE, ON JEAN HARLOW

. . . *a*lmost all the people sunning themselves on the sand were male and usually scantily clad, in that their trunks were the kind I used to call handkerchiefs full of apples. Seen from behind their buttocks mooned quite bare and strangely pale.

—GERMAINE GREER, *DADDY, WE HARDLY KNEW YOU*

*A*h, if I'd had breasts I could have ruled the world!

—JULIE HARRIS

*B*reasts had brought Jenny a peck of trouble over the years. With Patrick it was fair to say that they turned the scale. He seemed to stand up quite well to things like bottoms and faces, and she had heard him say more than once that he could take legs or leave them alone, which was rather sad, and tactless of him too, because her own were meant to be pretty good, one of her best features. But breasts were in a league of their own.

—KINGSLEY AMIS, *DIFFICULTIES WITH GIRLS*

*S*he wore a short skirt and a tight sweater and her figure described a set of parabolas that could cause cardiac arrest in a yak.

—WOODY ALLEN, *GETTING EVEN*

. . . *h*e twisted my nipples as though tuning a radio.

—LISA ALTHER, *KINFLICKS*

*B*ecause she had such a marvelous ass and because it was also so damned inaccessible I used to think of her as the Pons Asinorum. Every schoolboy knows that the

Pons Asinorum is not to be crossed except by two white donkeys led by a blind man.
—HENRY MILLER, *TROPIC OF CAPRICORN*

*T*he thrust of the buttocks, surely it was a little ridiculous. If you were a woman, and apart in all the business, surely that thrusting of the man's buttocks was supremely ridiculous. Surely the man was intensely ridiculous in this posture and this act!
—D. H. LAWRENCE, *LADY CHATTERLEY'S LOVER*

*"T*ha's got such a nice tail on thee," he said, in the throaty caressive dialect. "Tha's got the nicest arse of anybody. It's the nices woman's arse as it! An ivry bit of it woman, woman sure as nuts. Tha'rt not one o' them button-arsed lasses as should be lads, are ter! Tha's got a real sloping bottom on thee, as a man loves in 'is guts. It's a bottom as could hold the world up, it is."
—D. H. LAWRENCE, *LADY CHATTERLEY'S LOVER*

*O*f all the world's vistas, the one that cannot be surpassed is the female posterior.
—JOHN B. KEANE, ON IRISH TV

*F*ull-frontal nudity . . . has now become accepted by every branch of the theatrical profession with the possible exception of lady accordion-players.

—DENNIS NORDEN

*I*f it was the fashion to go naked, the face would be hardly observed.

—LADY MARY WORTLEY MONTAGU

*T*he bodies of most women are great works of art that go to pieces below the waist.

—ALEXANDER KING

*T*he brain is viewed as an appendage of the genital glands.

—CARL JUNG, ON FREUDIAN THEORY OF SEXUALITY

*I*f our elaborate and dominating bodies are given us to be denied at every turn, if our nature is always wrong and wicked, how ineffectual we are—like fishes not meant to swim.

—CYRIL CONNOLLY, *THE UNQUIET GRAVE*

*N*udist camps: Started by a group of sunbathers who, in their search for a perfect tan, were determined to leave no stern untoned.

—CHARLES DWELLY

*I*f monogamy is the height of all virtue then the palm goes to the tapeworm, which has a complete set of male and female sexual organs in each of its 50–200 proglottids of sections and spends its whole life copulating in all its sections with itself.

—FRIEDRICH ENGELS, *THE ORIGIN OF THE FAMILY*

*T*he trouble with nude dancing is that not everything stops when the music does.

—ROBERT HELPMAN

*A*ctually, if my business was legitimate, I would deduct a substantial percentage for depreciation of my body.

—XAVIERA HOLLANDER

*I*magine . . . hanging the stones of a man *outside,* where they are forever getting themselves knocked, pinched, and bruised. Any decent mechanic would have put them in the exact center of the body, protected by an envelope twice as thick as even a Presbyterian's skull. Moreover, consider certain parts of the female—always too large or too small. The elemental notion of standardization seems to have never presented itself to the celestial Edison.

—H. L. MENCKEN,
LETTER TO WILLIAM MANCHESTER

When she saw the sign "Members Only" she thought of him.

—SPIKE MILLIGAN, *PUCKOON*

No need to look at the mantlepiece when you're poking the fire.

—ENGLISH SAYING
(USED WHEN FORNICATING WITH AN UNATTRACTIVE WOMAN)

You know the worst thing about oral sex? The view.

—MAUREEN LIPMAN,
ENGLISH ACTRESS AND WRITER

*S*oon after leaving Amelia Island, I crossed my first state line into Georgia, leaving behind me the only state with an interesting silhouette on the map.

—NIGEL NICOLSON, *TWO ROADS TO DODGE CITY*

*M*any people may be depressed by the spectacle of naked humanity. Personally I can't see that an ugly body is any more offensive than an ugly dress.

—EVELYN WAUGH, *DAILY MAIL*

III. SEX IN MARRIAGE (AND ADULTERY)

"... the deep, deep peace of the double bed ..."

*W*edlock—the deep, deep peace of the double bed after the hurly-burly of the chaise-longue.

—MRS. PATRICK CAMPBELL

*M*en marry because they are tired; women because they are curious. Both are disappointed.

—OSCAR WILDE

*T*he reason why so few marriages are happy is because young ladies spend their time in making nets, not making cages.

—JONATHAN SWIFT

*M*arriage, if the current saying is true,
Has two good days—the first and the last.

—ALEXIS PERM

*H*e that get a wench with child and marry her afterwards, is as if a man should shit in his hat and then clap it on his head.

—SAMUEL PEPYS, *THE DIARY OF SAMUEL PEPYS*

*W*hen things don't work well in the bedroom, they don't work well in the living room either.
—Dr. William H. Masters,
Masters & Johnson Institute

———• •———

*L*iterature is mostly about sex and not much about having children and life is the other way round.
—David Lodge, *The British Museum Is Falling Down*

———• •———

A new bride should be treated like a new car. Keep her steady on straight, watch out for warning lights on

the ignition and lubrication panels and then when you reckon she's run in, give her all you've got.

—AUBERON WAUGH,
THE DIARIES OF AUBERON WAUGH

I don't see so much of Alfred any more since he got so interested in sex.

—MRS. ALFRED KINSEY

---

*L*ove, the quest; marriage the conquest; divorce, the inquest.

—HELEN ROWLAND

---

*T*he best sex education for kids is when Daddy pats Mommy on the fanny when he comes home from work.

—DR. WILLIAM H. MASTERS,
MASTERS & JOHNSON INSTITUTE

---

*M*arriage (whether registered or not) begins, not with setting up house, counting wedding presents, blowing kisses, looking at wedding groups, but with two bodies confronting one another like two wrestlers. To clinch and struggle and contend with one another. Rolling about, now one on top, now another; grunting, croaking,

sweating, murmuring, yelling. So the world began, with vast turbulence in the genitalia of space.
—MALCOLM MUGGERIDGE, *THE GREEN STICK*

*L*ove, for too many men of our time, consists of sleeping with a seductive woman, one who is properly endowed with the right distribution of curves and conveniences, and upon whom a permanent lien has been acquired through the institution of marriage.
—ASHLEY MONTAGU,
THE NATURAL SUPERIORITY OF WOMEN

*T*he main problem in marriage is that, for a man, sex is a hunger—like eating. If a man is hungry and can't get to a fancy French restaurant, he'll go to a hot dog stand. For a woman, what's important is love and romance.
—JOAN FONTAINE

*S*ex in marriage is like medicine. Three times a day for the first week. Then once a day for another week. Then once every three or four days until the condition clears up.
—PETER DEVRIES

I think the people who like sex stay home. I mean I don't think they make a big thing out of it.

—NELSON ALGREN

*S*ex is a momentary itch,
Love never lets you go.
—KINGSLEY AMIS,
AN EVER-FIXED MARK

*T*he way to a man's heart is through his wife's belly, and don't you forget it.

—EDWARD ALBEE,
WHO'S AFRAID OF VIRGINIA WOOLF?

*M*y wife doesn't. Understand me?

—ANONYMOUS

I've looked at a lot of women with lust. I've committed adultery in my heart many times.

—JIMMY CARTER, *PLAYBOY* INTERVIEW

I could not abide marriage, but as a rambler, I took a snatch when I could get it.

—ROBERT BURTON,
THE ANATOMY OF MELANCHOLY

ADDENDUM TO THE TEN COMMANDMENTS

*T*hou shalt not covet thy neighbor's wife,
Nor the ox her husband bought her;
But thank the Lord you're not forbidden
To covet your neighbor's daughter.
                    —ANONYMOUS

---

*H*e was one of those men who come in a door and make any woman with them look guilty.
                    —F. SCOTT FITZGERALD

I've only slept with men I've been married to. How many women can make that claim?
                    —ELIZABETH TAYLOR

---

*E*lizabeth's never been in a supermarket, in any kind of market. She's never in her life stood on line to use a public phone—a public anything. It's like deprivation. Elizabeth's a true innocent. Every time she gets laid, she gets married. Nobody ever told her you can do it and stay single . . . .
                    —LILLIAN HELLMAN,
          QUOTED BY PETER FEIBLEMAN IN *LILLY*

I say I don't sleep with married men, but what I mean is that I don't sleep with happily married men.

—BRITT EKLAND

*S*he could commit adultery at one end and weep for her sins at the other, and enjoy both operations at once.

—JOYCE CARY, *THE HORSE'S MOUTH*

*N*o *chupa,* no *shtupa*—no wedding, no bedding.

—YIDDISH PROVERB

*M*arriage is the price men pay for sex; sex is the price women pay for marriage.

—ANONYMOUS

*I*ntrigue here is the business of life, when a woman marries she throws off all restraint, but I believe their conduct is chaste enough before. If you make a proposal which in England would bring a box on the ear from the meekest of virgins to a Spanish girl, she thanks you for the honour you intend her, and replies, "Wait till I am married, & I shall be too happy."

—LORD BYRON

*A*dultery: second only to front-line combat, produces feats of almost lunatic daring. And it thrives on the extraordinary capacity of the deceived partner to ignore the signs of infidelity, so obvious to the rest of the world.

—MARY BEARD

*A*s a Jew, Jesus took seriously the Ten Commandments. But he totally confused the whole business of adultery by saying that even to entertain so much as a Carter-like lust for a woman is the equivalent of actually committing adultery.

—GORE VIDAL,
THE SECOND AMERICAN REVOLUTION

*E*ven a rat likes to go into a different hole once in a while.

—ANONYMOUS

I feel so guilty—he's my husband—he trusts me. If he didn't trust me I couldn't do this.

—ELAINE MAY,
IN SKETCH ABOUT AN ADULTEROUS WIFE

*F*RIAR BERNADINE: Thou hast committed adultery—
BARABAS: Fornication—but that was in another country; and besides, the wench is dead.

—CHRISTOPHER MARLOWE, *THE JEW OF MALTA*

*Y*ou can't tell your friend you've been cuckolded; even if he doesn't laugh at you, he may put the information to personal use.

—MONTAIGNE

*G*o, play, boy, play. There have been,
Or I am much deceived, cuckolds ere now,
And many a man there is (even at this present,

Now, while I speak this) holds his wife by th' arm,
That little thinks she has been sluic'd in's absence,
And his pond fish'd by his next neighbor—by
Sir Smile, his neighbor. Nay, there's comfort in't
Whiles other men have gates and those gates opened,
As mine, against their will. Should all despair
That have revolted wives, the tenth of mankind
Would hang themselves.
                              —SHAKESPEARE, *THE WINTER'S TALE*

*W*hat men call gallantry, and the gods adultery,
Is much more common where the climate's sultry.
                              —LORD BYRON, *DON JUAN*

"*N*ever Kiss a Married Woman on the Thigh"
                              —SHEL SILVERSTEIN, SONG TITLE

*A*dultery is a stimulant to men, but a sedative to women.
                              —MALCOLM DE CHAZAL, *PLASTIC SENSE*

*T*he woman who is adulterous in her home must always
remember one thing—put the seat down.
                              —WILLIAM COLE

*U*nfortunately, this world is full of people who are ready to think the worst when they see a man sneaking out of the wrong bedroom in the middle of the night.

—WILL CUPPY

IV. WOMEN ON MEN

"... with two legs and eight hands."

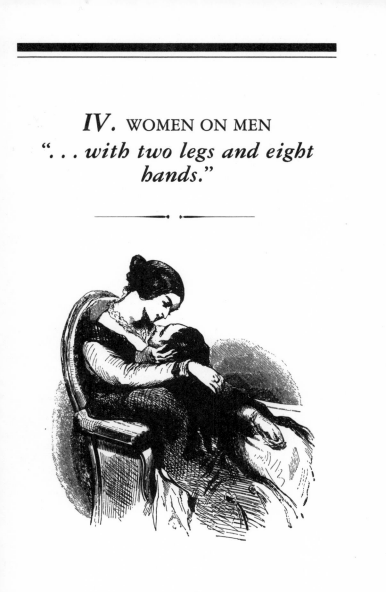

*M*en are those creatures with two legs and eight hands.
—JAYNE MANSFIELD

———• •———

*A*s lovers:

Americans	Fatherly and uncouth
French	Passionate and *petit maître*
Austrian	Sentimental and feckless
Hungarian	Passionate and exacting
Scandinavian	Psychological and scientific
Russian	Passionate and unstable
Spanish	Jealous and matter-of-fact
English	Casual and adorable
Italian	Romantic and fickle
German	Sentimental and vulgar
All the Near	Passionate and untrustworthy
East	—ELINOR GLYN

———• •———

I like to wake up each morning feeling a new man.
—JEAN HARLOW

———• •———

A many kisses he did give:
And I returned the same
Which made me willing to receive
That which I dare not name.
—APHRA BEHN, *"THE WILLING MISTRESS"*

*S*ex is first of all a very visual thing. A man walks through the door, and I think, yes I would, no I wouldn't. And any woman who says she doesn't think that way, at least for a second, is a liar.

—SORAYA KHASHOGGI, *WOMEN*

A gentleman is a patient wolf.

—HENRIETTA TIARKS

I wonder why men can get serious at all. They have this delicate long thing hanging outside their bodies, which goes up and down by its own will . . . . If I were a man I would always be laughing at myself.

—YOKO ONO, "ON FILM NO. 4,"
IN *GRAPEFRUIT*

*I*f the world were a logical place, men would ride side-saddle.

—RITA MAE BROWN

*G*ive a man a free hand, and he'll try to run it all over you.

—MAE WEST

*T*he worrying thing about sex is that the design of it is disturbing. It does tend to encourage the male to overwhelm the female, and the female reaction tends to be to want that to happen. The actual design has a flaw in it that brings on, at its worst, violence.

—MARY QUANT

*G*erman men always do things by the numbers. They seem to base their amorous advances on pages from a strange and misplaced book, a book that will never make the best seller charts here in America. They try to give you the impression that to accompany them from the airplane and share their bed would be a contribution toward some better, super-world.

—TRUDY BAKER AND RACHEL JONES,
COFFEE TEA OR ME

*M*en and women, women and men. It will never work.

—ERICA JONG

*M*en have been trained and conditioned by women, not unlike the way Pavlov conditioned his dogs, into becoming their slaves. As compensation for their labors men are given periodic use of women's vaginas.

—ESTHER VILAR

*D*on't accept rides from strange men—and remember that all men are strange as hell.

—ROBIN MORGAN

I like men to behave like men—strong and childish.

—FRANÇOISE SAGAN

*O*utside of every thin woman is a fat man trying to get in.

—KATHERINE WHITEHORN

*M*acho does not prove mucho.

—ZSA ZSA GABOR

*T*he male attitude toward sex is like squirting jam into a doughnut.

—GERMAINE GREER, *SEX AND DESTINY*

*T*he difference between a man and a turd is that after you've laid a turd you don't have to hug it.

—FEMINIST CHARACTER IN *STARING AT THE SUN* BY JULIAN BARNES

—*I* can't mate in captivity.

—GLORIA STEINEM, IN ANSWER TO THE QUESTION WHY SHE HAD NEVER MARRIED

*W*omen complain about sex more often than men. Their gripes fall into two major categories: (1) Not enough. (2) Too much.

—ANN LANDERS

*M*en make love more intensely at twenty, but make love better, however, at thirty.

—CATHERINE II OF RUSSIA

*O*nce you know what women are like, men get kind of boring. I'm not trying to put them down, I mean I like them sometimes as people, but sexually they're dull.

—RITA MAE BROWN

. . . *a*nd then I asked him with my eyes to ask again yes and then he asked me would I yes to say yes my mountain flower and first I put my arms around him yes and drew him down to me so he could feel my breasts all perfume yes and his heart was going like mad and yes I said yes I will Yes

—JAMES JOYCE, FROM MOLLY BLOOM'S
SOLILOQUY IN *ULYSSES*

*I*t would be less demanding, enslaving, perplexing and strenuous for a healthy male to screw a thousand women in his lifetime than to try to please one, and the potential for failure would be less.

—IRMA KURTZ, *MANTALK*

*G*eorge Moore unexpectedly pinched my behind. I felt rather honored that my behind should have drawn the attention of the great master of English Prose.

—ILKA CHASE

*B*oys don't make passes at female smart-asses.

—LETTY COTTIN POGREBIN

*M*en are so accustomed to lure, that one cannot take too many precautions before trusting them—if they are to be trusted at all.

—MARGUERITE DE VALOIS

*I*n real life, women are always trying to mix something up with sex—religion, babies, or hard cash; it is only men who long for sex separated out, without rings or strings.

—KATHERINE WHITEHORN

"... *m*an ... rushes to woman like the stag to the spring, and the woman to him like the threshing floor of the barn, shaken and heated by the many blows of the flail when the grain is threshed."

—HILDEGARDE VON BINGEN

A man needs the sexual conquest to prove that he can still do it, that he can still get it up. It's like having a duel with himself. He has to prove it all the time. We don't have to prove it. And very often we'll sleep with someone, not so much because we're turned on, but because we really want companionship, or we want the feeling of someone in bed with us.

—PRINCESS ELIZABETH OF YUGOSLAVIA,
IN *WOMEN*

A woman reading *Playboy* feels a little like a Jew reading a Nazi manual.

—GLORIA STEINEM

---

*I*f he has done nothing else for American culture, he has given it two of the great lies of the twentieth cen-

tury: "I buy it for the fiction" and "I buy it for the interview."

— NORA EPHRON,
ON *PLAYBOY*

---

*H*earst come, Hearst served.

— MARION DAVIES, MISTRESS OF
WILLIAM RANDOLPH HEARST

---

*W*omen fake orgasm if they really care about the man
because they don't want him to feel a sense of failure.
I think it's really a kind thing that women do. But they're
doing themselves an injustice, because probably, if they
could get over it, if they didn't fake it, and they learned
how to relax, they would probably have their orgasm.
Some men aren't good enough to give it to you.

— ANNIE FLANDERS, IN *WOMEN*

---

*M*uch contention and strife will arise in that house
where the wife shall get up dissatisfied with her husband.

— SA'DI, *GULISTAN*

I feel like a million tonight—but one at a time.

— MAE WEST

*T*he only place men want depth in women is in her décolletage.

—ZSA ZSA GABOR

*H*e's a fine writer, but I wouldn't want to shake hands with him.

—JACQUELINE SUSANN, ON PHILIP ROTH

*M*en ought to be more conscious of their bodies as an object of delight.

—GERMAINE GREER

*A*ll too many men still seem to believe, in a rather naive and egocentric way, that what feels good to them is automatically what feels good to women.

—SHERE HITE

*W*e still have these double standards where the emphasis is all on the male's sexual appetites—that it's OK for him to collect as many scalps as he can before he settles down and "pays the price." If a woman displays the same attitude, all the epithets that exist in the English language are laid at her door, and with extraordinary bitterness.

—GLENDA JACKSON

*F*or all the pseudo-sophistication of twentieth-century sex theory, it is still assumed that a man should make love as if his principal intention was to people the wilderness.

—GERMAINE GREER

*T*he desire engendered in the male gland is a hundred times more difficult to control than the desire bred in the female glands. All girls agreeing to a lovers' lane tête-á-tête in a car, knowing that they will limit their actions to arousing desires and then defend their "virtue," should be horsewhipped.

—MARLENE DIETRICH

I'm saving the bass player for Omaha.

—JANIS JOPLIN

*S*ex to Peter Rachman was like cleaning his teeth, and I was the toothpaste.

—CHRISTINE KEELER, FORMER CALL GIRL IN ENGLAND'S PROFUMO SCANDAL

*M*en need to be despunked regularly. It's when they're not getting a regular despunking that they start causing problems. I call that a service, not a nuisance.

—MADAME CYNTHIA PAYNE

V. MEN ON WOMEN
"Women are like banks, boy. . . ."

*W*omen are like banks, boy. Breaking and entering is
a serious business.
—JOE ORTON, *ENTERTAINING MR. SLOANE*

*T*HE CHEMICAL ANALYSIS OF WOMAN—
Thought to be a member of the human race. Seldom
found in natural state. Surface coated with paint and
other chemical compounds. Has low freezing point, but
also highly explosive. Extremely active when in the vicinity of opposite sex. Chiefly ornamental. Probably the
most powerful seducing agent known. Illegal to own
more than one specimen.
—ANONYMOUS

*I*t is naïve in the extreme for women to expect to be
regarded as equals by men . . . so long as they persist in
a subhuman (i.e., animal-like) behavior during sexual
intercourse. I'm referring . . . to the outlandish PANT-
ING, GASPING, MOANING, SOBBING, WRITH-
ING, SCRATCHING, BITING, SCREAMING con-
niptions, and the seemingly invariable "OH MY GOD
. . . OH MY GOD" all so predictably integral to pre-,
post-, and orgasmic stages of intercourse.
—TERRY SOUTHERN

*I*n Babylon, every respectable woman was obliged to
go at least once in a lifetime to the temple and prostitute

herself to the first pilgrim who was willing to pay her.
According to Herodotus, ill-favored women were
obliged to spend an awful lot of time at the temple,
trying to turn that reluctant trick which would make
them blessed in the eyes of the goddess.

—GORE VIDAL

*S*ir Henry Blount was called to the bar for spreading
abroad that abominable and dangerous doctrine that it
was far cheaper and safer to lie with common wenches
than with ladies of quality.

—JOHN AUBREY

I have heard the wish expressed that one could be a girl, and a goodlooking girl, between the ages of thirteen and twenty-two, and after that become a man.
—JEAN DE LA BRUYERE, *CHARACTERS*

I never turned over a figleaf that didn't have a price tag on the other side.
—SAUL BELLOW, ON *THE DICK CAVETT SHOW*

*S*ince maids, in modesty, say 'No' to that
Which they would have the profferer construe 'Aye.'
—SHAKESPEARE,
THE TWO GENTLEMEN OF VERONA

*T*hus woman's secrets I've surveyed
And let them see how curiously they're made,
And that, tho' they of different sexes be,
Yet on the whole they are the same as we.
For those that have the strictest searchers been,
Find women are but men turned outside in;
And men, if they but cast their eyes about,
May find they're women with their inside out.
—*THE WORKS OF ARISTOTLE
IN FOUR PARTS*, 1822 EDITION

*I*t would take a far more concentrated woman than Amanda to be unfaithful every five minutes.

—NOËL COWARD, *PRIVATE LIVES*

*T*he big mistake men make is that when they turn thirteen or fourteen and all of a sudden they've reached puberty, they believe that they like women. Actually, you're just horny. It doesn't mean you like women any more at twenty-one than you did at ten.

—JULES FEIFFER

*. . . a*s in the dark all Cats are grey, the Pleasure of corporeal Enjoyment with an old Woman is at least equal, and frequently superior, every Knack being by Practise capable of Improvement.

—BENJAMIN FRANKLIN

*O*lder women are best because they always think they may be doing it for the last time.

—IAN FLEMING

I trust you know the "three nevers" for proper gentlemen?

Never shoot south of the Thames
Never follow whisky with port
Never have your wife in the morning—the day may
   have something better to offer

—P. V. TAYLOR

*F*orget school kids: Why don't they bus horny women?

—GEORGE CARLIN

EPITAPH ON NELL GWYNN

*S*he was so exquisite a Whore,
That in the Belly of her Mother
Her Cunt was placed so right before,
Her father fucked them both together.
—JOHN WILMOT,
EARL OF ROCHESTER

---

*B*risk Confidence still best with woman copes:
Pique her and soothe in turn—soon Passion crowns thy
hopes.
—LORD BYRON, *CHILDE HAROLD'S PILGRIMAGE*

A girl's body in one's arms, its exciting nudity pro-
gressively disclosed: this has to be a figure of the male
heaven.

—ANTHONY BURGESS,
LITTLE WILSON AND BIG GOD

---

*N*o woman [is] so naked as one you can see to be naked
underneath her clothes.
—MICHAEL FRAYN

*T*he myth of the strong black woman is the other side of the coin of the myth of the beautiful dumb blonde. The white man turned the white woman into a weak-minded, weak-bodied, delicate freak, a sex pot, and placed her on a pedestal; he turned the black woman into a strong self-reliant Amazon and deposited her in his kitchen. . . . The white man turned himself into the Omnipotent Administrator and established himself in the Front Office.

—ELDRIDGE CLEAVER, "THE ALLEGORY OF
THE BLACK EUNUCHS," IN *SOUL ON ICE*

*I*n the case of some women, orgasms take quite a bit of time. Before signing on with such a partner, make sure you are willing to lay aside, say, the month of June, with sandwiches having to be brought in.

—BRUCE JAY FRIEDMAN

*T*o succeed with the opposite sex, tell her you're impotent. She can't wait to disprove it.

—CARY GRANT, AT AGE 72

*T*he old man, especially if he is in society, in the privacy of his thoughts, though he may protest the opposite, never stops believing that, through some singular exception of the universal rule, he can in some unknown and inexplicable way still make an impression on women.

—GIACOMO LEOPARDI, *PENSIERI*

I would say that the majority of women (happily for society) are not much troubled with sexual feeling of any kind.

—DR. WILLIAM ACTON, 1857

*I*t's a wise husband who keeps his own private chart foreseeing his wife's premenstrual snits.
—GARDNER E. LEWIS

*T*he great discovery of the age is that women like it too.
—HUGH MACDIARMID

. . . *b*efore D. H. Lawrence, Dr. [W. Somerset] Maugham (obstetrician) knew that women, given a fraction of a chance, liked sex as much as men did. When he said so, he was called a misogynist.
—GORE VIDAL,
IN *NEW YORK REVIEW OF BOOKS*

*W*omen now have the right to plant rolled-up dollar bills in the jockstraps of steroid-sodden male strippers.
—HOWARD OGDEN

*W*omen think of being a man as a gift. It is a duty. Even making love can be a duty. A man has always got to get it up, and love isn't always enough.
—NORMAN MAILER,
QUOTED IN *NOVA* MAGAZINE

*W*hen a man says he had pleasure with a woman he does not mean conversation.

—SAMUEL JOHNSON

*F*eminine passion is to masculine as an epic is to an epigram.

—KARL KRAUS

*N*o man should marry until he has studied anatomy and dissected at least one woman.

—HONORÉ DE BALZAC

*Y*ou have to do tobacco like you do women. You must let it work up to a good chew, let it get moist and juicy. If you chew too fast, it will become dry and fall apart.
—BASEBALL PLAYER PHIL GARNER

*T*he only way to resolve a situation with a girl is to jump on her and things will work out.
—LEE MARVIN, QUOTED IN *ESQUIRE*

*W*oman, observing that her mate went out of his way to make himself entertaining, rightly surmised that sex had something to do with it. From that she logically concluded that sex was recreational rather than pro-creational. (The small hardy band of girls who failed to get this point were responsible for the popularity of women's field hockey.)

—JAMES THURBER AND E. B. WHITE,
IS SEX NECESSARY?

---

*L*ady Capricorn, he understood, was still keeping open bed.

—ALDOUS HUXLEY, *ANTIC HAY*

I've been around so long I knew Doris Day before she was a virgin.

—GROUCHO MARX

---

*M*en are essentially dogs and women are essentially cats. Men are more capable of sniffing a new acquaint-ance's asshole on the sidewalk. Women are *sleeker.*

—MARTIN MULL, *THE CURMUDGEON'S GARDEN OF LOVE*

*W*hen a lady's erotic life is vexed
God knows what God is coming next.
—OGDEN NASH

*W*hen a woman becomes a scholar, there is usually
something wrong with her sex organs.

—NIETZSCHE

*T*here's really no reason to have a woman on a tour
unless they've got a job to do. The only other reason is
to screw. Otherwise they get bored, they just sit around
and moan.

—MICK JAGGER

*M*an regards woman with intellectual contempt and
sexual passion, both equally merited. Woman welcomes
the passion but resents the contempt. She wishes to be
rid of the discredit attached to her little brain, while
retaining the credit attached to her large bosom.

—A. E. HOUSMAN

*T*he evidence indicates that woman is, on the whole,
biologically superior to man.

—ASHLEY MONTAGU

*W*omen like brave men exceedingly, but audacious men still more.

—LEMESLES

*I*f men knew all that women think, they would be twenty times more audacious.

—ALPHONSE KARR

I don't like to admit it, but if a girl baited her trap with sex, she'd catch me every time—and it's unlikely this will ever cease to work.

—WILLIE NELSON,
WILLIE: AN AUTOBIOGRAPHY

VI. THE ACT ITSELF

". . . it cannot be called a dignified performance."

*W*hatever else can be said about sex, it cannot be called a dignified performance.

—HELEN LAWRENSON

*S*pring is hard on us;
Summer in bed we muss;
Fall the exploding beast;
Winter, post-coital triste.

—ANONYMOUS, TWENTIETH CENTURY

A contact of epidermises.

—FRENCH PROVERB

*A*t one time or another most men have had sexual encounters that have a sad similarity to pushing an oyster through a keyhole.

—ANONYMOUS

*M*arch isn't the only thing that's in like a lion, out like a lamb.

—ANONYMOUS

*T*he organ swelled and the bride came.

—AMERICAN CATCH PHRASE

*L*adies don't move.

—ENGLISH DICTUM

*I*f God made owt better, he made it for hisself.

—LANCASHIRE FOLK SAYING ABOUT SEX

*S*ex is dirty only when it's done right.

—WOODY ALLEN, *EVERYTHING YOU ALWAYS*
WANTED TO KNOW ABOUT SEX

*S*ex will always be better because it will always be dirty.

—FILMMAKER JOHN WATERS, EXPLAINING WHY
HE IS NOT UNHAPPY WITH HIS CATHOLIC BOYHOOD

I believe it was Galen who said that all animals are sad
after coitus except for the female human and the rooster.

—WILLIAM REDFIELD, *LETTERS FROM AN ACTOR*

*T*he orgasm has replaced the Cross as the focus of longing and the image of fulfillment.
—MALCOLM MUGGERIDGE,
THE MOST OF MALCOLM MUGGERIDGE

*H*oly Mother we do believe,
That without sin Thou didst conceive;
May we now in Thee believing,
Also sin without conceiving.
—A. P. HERBERT

*N*o sex is better than bad sex.

—GERMAINE GREER

*W*e know a west coast stewardess who was quite serious about a young Irish accountant but finally gave up.

"That business of crossing yourself every time gave me the creeps," she confesses. "I kept getting the feeling he was praying for me to perform good. Like a baseball player."

—TRUDY BAKER AND RACHEL JONES,
COFFEE TEA OR ME

You're not supposed to mention fucking in mixed company, and yet that's precisely the place you're supposed to do it.

—GEORGE CARLIN

I've tried several varieties of sex. The conventional position makes me claustrophobic. And other positions give me either a stiff neck or lockjaw.

—TALLULAH BANKHEAD,
QUOTED IN *PLAYBOY*

It's only human nature after all,
For a boy to get a girl against a wall
And slip his abomination into her accommodation
To increase the population of the coming generation.

—ENGLISH FOLK RHYME

The zipless fuck is absolutely pure . . . and it is rarer than the unicorn.

—ERICA JONG, *FEAR OF FLYING*

When the Prince of Wales, later to be King Edward VII, said to his mistress, Lily Langtry, during a quarrel, that "I've spent enough on you to buy a battleship," she replied, "And you've spent enough in me to float one."

. . . *t*he only hope of our ever getting a really beautiful and vigorous and charming civilization is to allow all the world to fuck and bugger and abuse themselves in public and generally misbehave to their heart's content.

—LYTTON STRACHEY

---

*T*he act of sex, gratifying as it may be, is God's joke on humanity. It is man's last desperate stand at superintendency.

—BETTE DAVIS, *THE LONELY LIFE*

---

*T*here are only two guidelines in good sex: "Don't do anything you don't really enjoy" and "Find out your partner's needs and don't balk them if you can help it."

—ALEX COMFORT

---

*T*here is no drama like the sexual drama: the sheer *effectiveness* of the human presentation and participation is overwhelming. Looked at as a spectacle in which one has one's *self* participating, it is the most entire delight that can be had.

—JAMES DICKEY

I may not be a great actress but I've become the greatest at screen orgasms. Ten seconds of heavy breathing, roll your head from side to side, simulate a slight asthma attack, and die a little.

—CANDICE BERGEN

*L*icense my roving hands and let them go
Before, behind, between, above, below.
Oh, my America, My Newfoundland.
—JOHN DONNE, "ELEGIE:
GOING TO BED"

*M*y own view, for what it's worth, is that sexuality is lovely, there cannot be too much of it, it is self-limiting if it is satisfactory, and satisfaction diminishes tension and clears the mind for attention and learning.

—PAUL GOODMAN, *COMPULSORY MISEDUCATION*

*T*he fact is there hasn't been a thrilling new erogenous zone discovered since de Sade.
—GEORGE GILDER, *SEXUAL SUICIDE*

*W*hoever loves, if he do not propose
The right true end of love, he's one that goes
To sea for nothing but to make him sick.
—JOHN DONNE, "ELEGIE: VARIETY"

*B*ut women also have their problems. Thus making love to a girl for the first time can be like going in-

to a dark room and fumbling for the electric switch. Only when a man has found it will the light come full on.

—GERALD BRENAN

*T*he true feeling of sex is that of a deep intimacy, but above all of a deep complicity.

—JAMES DICKEY

A skirt is no obstacle to extemporaneous sex, but it is physically impossible to make love to a girl while she is wearing trousers.

—HELEN LAWRENSON,
LATINS ARE STILL LOUSY LOVERS

*S*ex is a pleasurable exercise in plumbing, but be careful or you'll get yeast in your drain tap.

—RITA MAE BROWN

*C*harles himself was not an imperious lover. Calm and svelte, stealthy as a cat in his movements, he seemed to approach sex as a form of research, favoring techniques of foreplay so subtle and prolonged that Robyn occasionally dozed off in the middle of them, and would wake with a guilty start to find him still crouched studiously over her body, fingering it like a box of index cards.

—DAVID LODGE, *NICE WORK*

*T*he Duke returned from the wars today and did pleasure me in his top-boots.

—SARAH, DUCHESS OF MARLBOROUGH

*L*ove is not the dying moan of a distant violin—it's the triumphant twang of a bedspring.

—S. J. PERELMAN

*H*e said it was artificial respiration but now I find I'm to have his child.

—ANTHONY BURGESS, *INSIDE MR ENDERBY*

*W*e have long passed the Victorian Era when asterisks were followed at a certain interval by a baby.

—W. SOMERSET MAUGHAM,
THE CONSTANT WIFE

*C*ontraceptives should be used on every conceivable occasion.

—SPIKE MILLIGAN

I like making love myself and I can make love for about *three minutes*. Three minutes of serious fucking and I need eight hours sleep, and a bowl of Wheaties.

—RICHARD PRYOR

*I*f you aren't going all the way, why go at all?

—JOE NAMATH

*I*f I don't do it every day, I get a headache.
—WILLIE NELSON, *WILLIE: AN AUTOBIOGRAPHY*

---

*Y*our daughter and the Moor are now making the beast with two backs.

—SHAKESPEARE, *OTHELLO*

. . . *C*hasing the naughty couples down the grassgreen gooseberried double bed of the wood. . . .
—DYLAN THOMAS, *UNDER MILK WOOD*

---

*S*ince copulation is the most important act in the lives of living creatures because it perpetuates the species, it seems odd that nature should not have arranged it to happen more simply.
—GERALD BRENAN, *THOUGHTS IN A DRY SEASON*

VII. MASTURBATION AND PERVERSIONS

". . . with someone I love."

*D*on't knock masturbation. It's sex with someone I love.

—WOODY ALLEN, *ANNIE HALL*

"*W*ith whom did you first do it?"
"I was alone at the time."

—WOODY ALLEN

*T*he nice thing about masturbation is that you don't have to dress up for it.

—ATTRIBUTED TO TRUMAN CAPOTE

"*S*omeday My Prince Will Come," said Snow White, changing hands for the fifth time.

—ENGLISH CATCH PHRASE

*I*t is called in our schools "beastliness," and this is about the best name for it . . . should it become a habit it quickly destroys both health and spirits, he becomes feeble in body and mind, and often ends in a lunatic asylum.

—LORD BADEN-POWELL

I'll come and make love to you at five o'clock. If I'm late start without me.

—TALLULAH BANKHEAD, QUOTED IN
SOMERSET MAUGHAM BY TED MORGAN

*M*arilyn Monroe was a masturbation-fantasy of bell-boys; Grace Kelly of bank executives.

—JAMES DICKEY

*T*he world is full of double beds
And such delightful maidenheads
That there is simply no excuse
For sodomy and self-abuse.

—HILAIRE BELLOC

*M*asturbation: the primary sexual activity of mankind. In the nineteenth century it was a disease; in the twentieth, it's a cure.

—THOMAS SZASZ

I knew nothing at all about sex and simply thought that masturbation was a unique discovery on my part that was a lonely hobby of a sort that produced a pleasant sensation. I introduced it to my incredibly innocent prep school the next term—feeling like Marco Polo returning to Europe with the new inventions of gunpowder and paper—and soon the entire school was rocked to its foundations both metaphorically and physically.

—JEFFREY BERNARD, *LOW LIFE*

*I*f God had intended us not to masturbate, He would have made our arms shorter.

—GEORGE CARLIN

I believe that sex is a beautiful thing between two people. Between *five,* it's fantastic.

—WOODY ALLEN

*Y*ou get a better class of person at orgies, because people have to keep in trim more. There is an awful lot of going round holding in your stomach, you know. Everybody is very polite to each other. The conversation isn't very good but you can't have everything.

—GORE VIDAL

*I*f God had meant us to have group sex, he'd have given us more organs.

—MALCOLM BRADBURY

*T*o the lonely it is company; to the forsaken it is a friend; to the aged and the impotent it is a benefactor; they that are penniless are yet rich, in that they still have this majestic diversion.

—CAESAR, *COMMENTARIES*, QUOTED BY MARK TWAIN, IN SPEECH "THE SCIENCE OF ONANISM"

*O*h, my sister's name is Tilly,
She's a whore in Picadilly,
And my mother is another in The Strand.
And my brother peddles arsehole
At the Elephant and Castle
We're the finest fucking family in the land.
—LONDON FOLK RHYME

---

*T*here is no unhappier creature on earth than a fetishist who yearns for a woman's shoe and has to embrace the whole woman.

—KARL KRAUS,
APHORISMS AND MORE APHORISMS

---

*S*exual perversions are as infectious as venereal disease and are passed from one person to another. This is especially true of sadomasochism.

—GERALD BRENAN

---

*N*onspontaneous sex is creepy, boring, and passé. Practitioners of sport call themselves "swingers." (I ask you.) Swingers are all from the suburbs and consequently brain-addled by car pools, shopping malls, and welcome wagons. Swinger men affect furtive eyes and oozing glutinous voices. Swinger women wear complicated hairdos and sheepish expressions.

—CYNTHIA HEIMEL, *SEX TIPS FOR GIRLS*

———— ∙ ∙ ————

I'm at the age where food has taken the place of sex in my life. In fact, I've just had a mirror put over my kitchen table.

—RODNEY DANGERFIELD

———— ∙ ∙ ————

I am a strict monogamist: it is twenty years since I last went to bed with two women at once, and then I was in my cups and not myself.

—H. L. MENCKEN

———— ∙ ∙ ————

*S*ex between a man and a woman can be wonderful—provided you get between the right man and the right woman.

—WOODY ALLEN

———— ∙ ∙ ————

*T*here is an ineradicable bond between two men who have made love to the same woman—at the same time.

—WILLIAM COLE

*D*ear Earthling,

Hi! I am a bisexual creature from outer space. I have transformed myself into this postal card. Right now, I am having sex with your fingers. I know you like it because you are smiling. Please pass me on to someone else. . . .

—ANONYMOUS POSTCARD RECEIVED BY
PAUL DICKSON, *THE NEW OFFICIAL RULES*

I'm all for bringing back the birch, but only between consenting adults.

—GORE VIDAL

*W*hat is wrong with a little incest? It is both handy and cheap.

—JAMES AGATE, REVIEWING *THE BARRETTS
OF WIMPOLE STREET*

*I*f it weren't for pickpockets, I'd have no sex life at all.

—RODNEY DANGERFIELD

*I*t is very disturbing indeed when you can't think of any new perversions that you would like to practise.

—JAMES DICKEY

*C*hastity is the most unnaturual of the sexual perversions.

—REMY DE GOURMONT

VIII. HOMOSEXUALITY OF VARIOUS KINDS

"...don't frighten the horses."

*I*t doesn't matter what the dear boys do so long as they don't do it in the street and frighten the horses.
—MRS. PATRICK CAMPBELL

*A*h, yes, there's Micheál MacLiammóir, up to the Hilton Edwards.
—IRISH WISECRACK, REFERRING TO NOTED
THEATRICAL COUPLE
(SOMETIMES REFERRED TO AS "SODOM AND BEGORRAH")

*S*plendid couple—slept with both of them.
—ATTRIBUTED TO SIR MAURICE BOWRA, ON THE
WEDDING OF A WELL-KNOWN LITERARY COUPLE

*S*weetest li'l feller,
Everybody knows;
Dunno what to call him,
But I think he's one of those . . .
—ENGLISH MUSIC HALL SONG
TO THE TUNE OF "MIGHTY LAK A ROSE"

*T*here are lots of easier things in this life than being a drag queen, but I ain't got no choice. The fact is I just can't walk in flats.
—HARVEY FIERSTEIN, *TORCH SONG TRILOGY*

*I*n England the vices in fashion are whoring and drink-
ing, in Turkey, sodomy and smoking, we prefer a girl
and a bottle, they a pipe and a pathic.

—LORD BYRON

*I*t is a perfectly ordinary little case of a man charged
with indecency with four or five guardsmen.

—MERVYN GRIFFITHS-JONES,
PROSECUTING COUNSEL

I was asked if my first sexual experience was homosexual or heterosexual. I said I was too polite to ask.

—GORE VIDAL

*A*nd we have boys and girls of special kinds,
  White, brown and black, fragile or fair or strong;
Their bosoms shame the roses: their behinds
  Impel the astonished nightingales to song.

—JAMES ELROY FLECKER, *Hassan*

I'm a practising heterosexual, but bisexuality immediately doubles your chances for a date on Saturday night.

—WOODY ALLEN

*B*isexuality is not so much a copout as a fearful compromise.

—JILL JOHNSTON

*I*n Suburbia they thump you for anything. . . . People still think heteros make love and gays have sex. I want to tell them that's wrong.

—BOY GEORGE
(ALAN O'DOWD)

I want more in life than meeting a pretty face and sitting down on it.
—HARVEY FIERSTEIN, *TORCH SONG TRILOGY*

I became one of the stately homos of England.
—QUENTIN CRISP

*T*he worst part of being gay in the twentieth century is all that damn disco music to which one has to listen.
—QUENTIN CRISP, *MANNERS FROM HEAVEN*

I discarded a whole book because the leading character wasn't on my wavelength. She was a lesbian with doubts about her masculinity.
—PETER DEVRIES

*T*he Irish queer was cynically defined as a man who preferred women to drink. It might be redefined as a man who preferred women to talking.
—DAVID HANLEY

*T*he problem which confronts homosexuals is that they set out to win the love of a "real" man. If they succeed they fail. A man who "goes with" other men is not what they would call a real man.

—QUENTIN CRISP, *THE NAKED CIVIL SERVANT*

*S*ome of the happiest marriages, in fact, are when homosexuals marry upper-class ladies, a kind of "with my buddy, I thee worship." The sex works, because the upper-class woman doesn't expect much, and the man just shuts his eyes and thinks of Benjamin Britten.

—JILLY COOPER

*. . . O*n Fire Island . . . the atmosphere is sick, sick, sick. Never in my life have I seen such concentrated, abandoned homosexuality. It is fantastic and difficult to believe. . . . Thousands of queer young men of all shapes and sizes camping about blatantly and carrying on—in my opinion—appallingly. Then there were all the lesbians glowering at each other. . . . I have always been of the opinion that a large group of queer men was unattractive. In Fire Island it is more than unattractive, it's macabre, sinister, irritating and somehow tragic.

—NOËL COWARD, *DIARIES*

*T*here has been another high-flown debate in the House of Lords about suggested (idiotic) amendments to the Homosexual Bill, in the course of which Lord Montgomery announced that homosexuality between men was the most abominable and beastly act that any human being could commit! It, in his mind, apparently compares unfavorably with disembowelling, torturing, gas chambers and brutal murder. It is inconceivable that a man of his eminence and achievements could make such a statement. The poor old sod must be gaga.

—NOËL COWARD, *DIARIES*

*T*his sort of thing may be tolerated by the French— but we are British, thank God.

—VISCOUNT MONTGOMERY, HOUSE OF LORDS

*I*f homosexuality were the normal way God would have made Adam and Bruce.

—ANITA BRYANT

*D*o you know why God hates homosexuality? Because the male homosexual eats another man's sperm. Sperm is the most concentrated form of blood. The homosexual is eating life.

—ANITA BRYANT

*H*omosexuality is a sickness, just as are baby-rape or wanting to become head of General Motors.
—ELDRIDGE CLEAVER, *NOTES OF A NATIVE SON*

I would rather put a phial of prussic acid in the hand of a healthy boy or girl than the book in question.
—JAMES DOUGLAS, LITERARY CRITIC OF THE
LONDON SUNDAY EXPRESS, COMMENTING ON
THE WELL OF LONELINESS
BY RADCLYFFE HALL

*E*verything is controlled by the sods. The country is riddled with homosexuals who are teaching the world how to behave—a spectacle of revolting hypocrisy.
—SIR THOMAS BEECHAM, QUOTED IN THE BIOGRAPHY OF HIM BY CHARLES REED

*F*airies: Nature's attempt to get rid of soft boys by sterilizing them.
—F. SCOTT FITZGERALD, *THE CRACK-UP*

I thought men like that shot themselves!
—GEORGE V, ON HOMOSEXUALS

*W*e're here because we're queer
Because we're queer because we're here.
—BRENDAN BEHAN, *THE HOSTAGE*

*T*chaikovsky thought of committing suicide for fear of being discovered as a homosexual; but today, if you are a composer and *not* a homosexual, you might as well put a bullet through your head.
—DIAGHILEV

*T*here are three kinds of pianists: Jewish pianists, homosexual pianists, and bad pianists.
—VLADIMIR HOROWITZ

*B*uggery is spiritually valuable because of its difficulties and torments.
—W. H. AUDEN, QUOTED IN THE BIOGRAPHY OF HIM BY HUMPHREY CARPENTER

*A*merica has the longest prison sentences in the West, yet the only condition long sentences demonstrably cure is heterosexuality.
—PROFESSOR BRUCE JACKSON, STATE UNIVERSITY OF NEW YORK AT BUFFALO

*T*here's nothing wrong with going to bed with somebody of your own sex. People should be very free with sex—they should draw the line at goats.
—ELTON JOHN

*H*omosexuality is the new French Foreign Legion.
—FLORENCE KING

. . . *a*t least British actors, unlike their American counterparts, do not embrace you. I loathe being hugged by a man; there is always the lurking fear of someday meeting one who will not let go.

—HUGH LEONARD

*T*he middle age of buggers is not to be contemplated without horror.

—VIRGINIA WOOLF

*T*here is probably no sensitive heterosexual alive who is not preoccupied with his latent homosexuality.

—NORMAN MAILER, *ADVERTISEMENTS FOR MYSELF*

*M*ost of my male friends are gay, and that seems perfectly natural to me. I mean, who wouldn't like a cock?

—VALERIE PERRINE

*T*he love that previously dared not speak its name has now grown hoarse from screaming.

—ROBERT BRUSTEIN

*T*he love that dare not speak its name has become the neurosis that does not know when to shut up.

—*TIME* MAGAZINE

*I*t is interesting to know that Wilde, unlike Byron, Charlemagne and Lassie, was not into buggery, preferring either oral sex or the Dover-sole kiss *cum* inter-crural friction.

—GORE VIDAL

Nancy Mitford had the distinction of being one of the first "fag hags," since she revelled in the company of effeminate young men.

— PETER ACKROYD, THE LONDON SUNDAY *TIMES*

Girls who put out are tramps. Girls who don't are ladies. This is, however, a rather archaic use of the word. Should one of you boys happen upon a girl who doesn't put out, do not jump to the conclusion that you have found a lady. What you have probably found is a lesbian.

— FRAN LIEBOWITZ, *METROPOLITAN LIFE*

If I were asked to describe the difference between the sexes in the gay world, I would say that the men wanted to be amused; the girls sought vindication.

— QUENTIN CRISP

Afterwards, you know, afterwards, I often feel like being fucked by a man, too. . . . You *tune* me, d'you see, and then I want a man to counter me, but we together, we just keep traveling to strung out space. We can't comfort each other.

— JOAN HAGGERTY, *DAUGHTERS OF THE MOON*

*T*hank you, Agatha, for the lovely bracelet, but I still haven't changed my mind. I have no desire to touch you in places that I already own. Sincerely, Sheila Levine.
—GAIL PARENT, *SHEILA LEVINE IS DEAD AND LIVING IN NEW YORK*

i never said i was a dyke even to a dyke because there wasn't a dyke in the land who thought she should be a dyke or even thought she was a dyke so how could we talk about it.
—JILL JOHNSTON, *LESBIAN NATION: THE FINAL SOLUTION*

*M*any years ago I chased a woman for almost two years, only to discover her tastes were exactly like mine: We were both crazy about girls.
—GROUCHO MARX

*T*wo men—yes—I can see they've got something to take hold of. But two women—that's impossible. You can't have two insides having an affair!
—LYDIA LOPOKOVA

IX. QUIPS, CRACKS, AND ODDITIES
"I used to be Snow White . . ."

I used to be Snow White, but I drifted.

—MAE WEST

PALINDROMES

*E*ROS? SIDNEY, MY END IS SORE!
A SLUT NIXES SEX IN TULSA
SEX AT NOON TAXES
EGAD! NO BONDAGE!
DENNIS AND EDNA SINNED
NAOMI, DID I MOAN?

And a word-by-word palindrome, created by Gerald
Benson. Published in the *New Statesman & Nation*.

"Come, shall I stroke your 'whatever,' darling? I am so
randy." "So am I, darling. Whatever your stroke, I shall
come."

GRAFFITI

*T*o go together is blessed; to come together is divine
Accidents cause people
It's not the length of the wand, but the finesse of the
   magician that puts the rabbit in the hat
I am twelve inches long and three inches around.
   . . . and under it: Great. How big is your penis?

Bionic man can't get it down
Vasectomy means never having to say you're sorry
Don't let your meat loaf
Leda loves swans
(sign in a bar) Liquor in the front, poker in the rear
One orgasm in the bush is worth two in the hand
Oedipus was a motherfucker
Graffito for a German virgin who sneezes: "Goesintight!"
God is looking at your pussy.

*T*here are few virtuous women who are not weary of
their profession.

—LA ROCHEFOUCAULD

I tend to believe that cricket is the greatest thing God ever created on earth . . . certainly greater than sex, although sex isn't too bad either.

—HAROLD PINTER

---

*O*ne finger professionally, gentlemen; two fingers socially.

—GYNECOLOGIST'S SAYING

---

*I*n 1945 an Italian-English phrase book was hastily compiled in Florence to promote a better understanding between the Florentines and British and American troops. It contained the following entry:

ITALIAN	ENGLISH
Posso presentare il conte.	Meet the cunt.

—W. H. AUDEN, *A CERTAIN WORLD*

---

*A*lthough written many years ago, *Lady Chatterley's Lover* has just been reissued by Grove Press, and this fictional account of the day-by-day life of an English game-keeper is still of considerable interest to outdoor-minded readers, as it contains many passages on pheasant-raising, the apprehending of poachers, ways to control vermin, and other chores and duties of the professional game-keeper.

Unfortunately, one is obliged to wade through many pages of extraneous material in order to discover and savor these sidelights on the management of a Midland shooting estate, and in this reviewer's opinion the book cannot take the place of J. R. Miller's *Practical Game-keeper.*

—BOOK REVIEW FROM THE AMERICAN MAGAZINE,
FIELD & STREAM

I would rather go to bed with Lillian Russell stark naked than Ulysses S. Grant in full military regalia.

—MARK TWAIN

---

*T*he marines' chosen name for their female aides is *bams,* from *big-assed,* or *broad-assed, marines.* The marine major said that the Washington philologians are now wrestling with the embarrassing problem of inventing an abbreviation for Columbia University Nurses Training-school. The initial letters, of course, would not do at all.

—H. L. MENCKEN, *DIARIES*

---

*P*erhaps the heaviest cross any company has to bear was what the Street called the old Fairbanks Morse

stock, whose symbol before the company vanished into Colt Industries was FKM. Recently, FKM reappeared on the Amex tape, and word spread like lightning around the Street that "FKM is back." The new butt of it all: Fluke Mfg. Co.

—*Business Week*

*P*rostitution gives her an opportunity to meet people. It provides fresh air and wholesome exercise, and it keeps her out of trouble.

—Joseph Heller, *Catch 22*

*H*e offered his honor
She honored his offer,
And all through the night
He was on her and off her.
　　　—AMERICAN FOLK RHYME

*B*usts and bosoms have I known
Of various shapes and sizes,
From grievous disappointments
To jubilant surprises.
　　　　—AMERICAN FOLK RHYME

I suspect that one of the reasons we create fiction is to make sex exciting.

　　　　　　　—GORE VIDAL

*T*emptation, temptation, temptation,
Dick Barton went down to the station,
Blondie was there, all naked and bare,
Temptation, temptation, temptation . . .
　　　　—ENGLISH CHILDREN'S RHYME

*H*ooray! Hooray!
The first of May;
Outdoor screwing
Begins today!
—AMERICAN FOLK RHYME

*C*ontinental people have sex life; the English have hot-water bottles.

—GEORGE MIKES

*W*hen I was young, I used to have successes with women because I was young. Now I have successes with women because I am old. Middle age was the hardest part.

—ARTHUR RUBENSTEIN

*B*eing with a woman all night never hurt no professional baseball player. It's staying up all night looking for a woman that does him in.

—CASEY STENGEL

I've got nothing against sex, it's a marvelous human activity, but it was watching others do it all the time that got me down.

—JOHN TREVELYAN, ON WHY HE RESIGNED AS A BRITISH FILM CENSOR

*A*cting is not very hard. The most important things are to be able to laugh and cry. If I have to cry, I think of my sex life. And if I have to laugh, well, I think of my sex life.

—GLENDA JACKSON

*O*ne more drink and I'll be under the host.
　　　　　　　　　　　　　—DOROTHY PARKER

*I*f all the girls attending the Yale-Harvard game were laid end to end, I wouldn't be at all surprised.
　　　　　　　　　　　　　—DOROTHY PARKER

*T*he French they are a funny race,
Parlez vous;
They fight with their feet and they fuck with their face,
Hinky dinky *parlez vous.*
　　　　　　　　　　　　　—WORLD WAR I SONG

*O*ld Mother Hubbard
Went to the cupboard
To get her poor doggie a bone;
But when she bent over
Rover drove her,
For Rover had a bone of his own.
　　　　　　　　　　　　　—AMERICAN PARODY

*H*e's everything I'm not. He's young; he's beautiful; he has lots of hair; he's fast; he's durable; he has a large bank account; and his entire sex life is before him.
—SI BURICK, WHEN THE HORSE SECRETARIAT WAS
　　　　　　　　　　　RETIRED TO STUD

*T*ell him I've been too fucking busy—or vice versa.
—DOROTHY PARKER, WHEN ASKED WHY SHE HAD
NOT DELIVERED HER COPY ON TIME

*D*ucking for apples—change one letter and it's the story of my life.

—DOROTHY PARKER

I hate a woman who offers herself because she ought to do so, and, cold and dry, thinks of her sewing when she's making love.

—OVID, *THE ART OF LOVE*

*A*s to sex, the original pleasure, I cannot recommend too highly the advantages of androgyny.

—JAN MORRIS

*A*s Abe Martin says, women is just like elephants; I like to look at 'em, but I'd sure hate to own one.

—WILL ROGERS

*A*mazing! Astonishing! Still can't get over the fantastic idea that when you are looking at a girl, you are looking

at somebody who is guaranteed to have on her—a cunt!
They *all* have *cunts!* Right under their dresses! Cunts—
for fucking!

—PHILIP ROTH, *PORTNOY'S COMPLAINT*

*P*rostitution seems to be a problem. But what's the
problem? Fucking is okay. Selling is okay. So why isn't
selling fucking okay?

—GEORGE CARLIN

*I*t is odd that neither the Church nor modern public
opinion condemns petting, provided it stops short at a
certain point. At what point sin begins is a matter to
which casuists differ. One eminently orthodox Catholic
divine laid it down that a confessor may fondle a nun's
breasts, provided he does it without evil intent. But I
doubt whether modern authorities would agree with him
on this point.

—BERTRAND RUSSELL, *UNPOPULAR ESSAYS*

I was thinking one night about the words you wouldn't
say on the public, ah, airwaves, um, the words you
wouldn't say ever . . . the original seven words were:
shit, piss, fuck, cunt, cocksucker, motherfucker, and tits.
Those are the ones that will curve your spine, grow hair

on your hand, and maybe even bring us, God help us, peace without honor . . . .
—FROM A TRANSCRIPT PREPARED BY THE FEDERAL COMMUNICATIONS COMMISSION OF THE GEORGE CARLIN "FILTHY WORDS" MONOLOGUE ON WBAI-FM, NEW YORK CITY

*I*t has to be admitted that we English have sex on the brain, which is a very unsatisfactory place to have it.
—MALCOLM MUGGERIDGE

I keep making up these sex rules for myself and then I break them right away.
—HOLDEN CAULFIELD IN J. D. SALINGER'S *THE CATCHER IN THE RYE*

*G*reat food is like great sex—the more you have the more you want.
—GAEL GREEN

*T*oo much of a good thing can be wonderful.
—MAE WEST

I will find you twenty lascivious turtles ere one chaste man.
—SHAKESPEARE, *THE MERRY WIVES OF WINDSOR*

*D*espite a lifetime of service to the cause of sexual liberation I have never caught a venereal disease, which makes me feel rather like an arctic explorer who has never had frostbite.
—GERMAINE GREER IN *THE OBSERVER*

. . . *M*rs. Sanger's pamphlet on birth control, which is addressed to working women, was declared obscene on the ground that working women could understand it. Dr. Marie Stopes's books, on the other hand, are not illegal, because their language can only be understood by persons with a certain amount of education. The consequence is that, while it is permissible to teach birth control to the well-to-do, it is criminal to teach it to wage-earners and their wives.
—BERTRAND RUSSELL, *UNPOPULAR ESSAYS*

*I*f I had as many love affairs as you have given me credit for, I would now be speaking to you from a jar in the Harvard Medical School.
—FRANK SINATRA, AT A PRESS CONFERENCE

"You know what I like about having you come in my mouth? I feel like a blind person—you know how they say blind people feel with their faces so they can practically see a building? Same thing. . . . Now I've felt it this way, the next time you come in my cunt I'll practically see it. . . ."
—JOHN CASEY, FEMALE CHARACTER SPEAKING IN HIS NOVEL, *SPARTINA*

You gotta learn that if you don't get it by midnight, chances are you ain't gonna get it; and if you do, it ain't worth it.

—CASEY STENGEL

I'll wager you that in ten years it will be fashionable again to be a virgin.
—BARBARA CARTLAND, IN *THE OBSERVER*

Never miss a chance to have sex or appear on television.
—GORE VIDAL

. . . for many women, anyhow for me, passion is independent of the sex machine. Of course when you are young, it will not be gainsaid. (Nor indeed, if I am frank,

did it cease to play any part with me when I should have
done with all things physical.)

—DAME ETHEL SMYTH, *MEMOIRS*

*I*t was not the apple tree, but the pair on the ground,
I believe, that caused the trouble in the garden.

— M. D. O'CONNOR

I've tried everything but coprophagia and necrophilia,
and I like kissing best.

—JOHN WATERS

*W*hat holds the world together, I have learned from bitter experience, is sexual intercourse.
—HENRY MILLER, *TROPIC OF CAPRICORN*

*T*he late, alas, Maurice Bowra—and how one misses that ebullient, generous, warm, witty, and hilarious fellow—used to insist that there existed a City firm of solicitors called Mann, Rogers and Greaves—the history of the world in a nutshell.
—ARTHUR MARSHALL, *TAKING LIBERTIES*

*N*ature abhors a virgin—a frozen asset.
—CLARE BOOTH LUCE

*I*t nearly broke the family's heart
When Lady Jane became a tart,
But pride is pride, and race is race,
And so, to save the family's face,
They bought her a most exclusive beat
On the sunny side of Jermyn Street.
—ENGLISH FOLK RHYME

*W*hat is a promiscuous person? It's usually someone who is getting more sex than you are.
—VICTOR LOWNES

A sex symbol becomes a thing. I hate being a thing.
—MARILYN MONROE

---

*N*iagara Falls is only the second biggest disappointment of the standard honeymoon.
—OSCAR WILDE

---

*M*urder is a crime. Describing murder is not. Sex is not a crime. Describing sex is.
—GERSHON LEGMAN

---

*L*enny Bruce got arrested for saying cocksucker in the sixties, but Meryl Streep got an Academy Award for saying it in the eighties.
—PAUL KRASSNER

---

*T*o have a new mistress is a pleasure only surpassed by that of ridding yourself of an old one.
—WILLIAM WYCHERLEY

---

*T*he cure for starvation in India *and* the cure for overpopulation—both in one big swallow.
—ERICA JONG, *FEAR OF FLYING*

*I*t was love on the run with half the buttons undone. The results were like a high-speed film—blurrin' but excitin'.
—MAE WEST, ON A LOVE AFFAIR WITH GEORGE RAFT

---

*Y*ou were born with your legs apart. They'll send you to your grave in a Y-shaped coffin.
—JOE ORTON, *WHAT THE BUTLER SAW*

---

*C*unning Stunts
English woman's entertainment group

The Slits
           All-women, new wave English rock band

———————

*E*verybody is trying to convince people that kids are interested in ecology, that kids are interested in politics. That's bullshit. Kids are interested in the same things that have always excited them: sex and violence.
                                    —ALICE COOPER

———————

*A*mong the porcupines, rape is unknown.
                                    —GREGORY CLARK

———————

*A*s soon as sex comes up we collectively say "Er . . ." instead of "Aha!"
                          —WAYLAND YOUNG, BRITISH POLITICIAN

———————

*T*he kiss originated when the first male reptile licked the first female reptile, implying in a subtle, complimentary way that she was as succulent as the small reptile he had had for dinner the night before.
                  —F. SCOTT FITZGERALD, *THE NOTEBOOKS*

*V*ery smart stomach dancers and men dancers and delicious mint tea, and O so funny, they sprinkle you with rose water and also bring along a silver brazier of incense and cedar, and put it under the ladies' skirts. You are then invited to put your nose under your dress between your breasts and inhale. You can imagine how some of the old English girls dealt with the situation and what an extraordinarily indecent effect the operation gave.
—DIANA DUFF COOPER, LETTER TO DUFF COOPER,
A DURABLE FIRE

A lot of time has been wasted on arguing over which came first—the chicken or the egg. It was undoubtedly the rooster.
—AMBASSADOR THEODORE C. ACHILLES,
IN *THE NEW OFFICIAL RULES* BY PAUL DICKSON

*T*here goes a good time that was had by all.
—BETTE DAVIS, REMARKING ON A PASSING STARLET

I want to tell you a terrific story about oral contraception. I asked this girl to sleep with me and she said "no."
—WOODY ALLEN

*I*f you've been around at all you know that female teachers rank among the world's greatest swingers. Put a knowledgeable guy in a bar loaded with women of different backgrounds and he'll head for the teacher. He knows.

—TRUDY BAKER AND RACHEL JONES,
COFFEE TEA OR ME

---

*E*ven the simple wing sounds of midges and mosquitos play a role in bringing the sexes together. In this case it is the female that attracts the male by the hum of her wings, a fact quite quickly apparent to singers who hit a G in the vicinity of a swarm and end up with a mouthful of mosquitos.

—PROFESSOR HOWARD EVANS OF FORT COLLINS, COLORADO, IN *CHRISTMAS CRACKERS*

---

*M*oney, it turned out, was exactly like sex, you thought of nothing else if you didn't have it and thought of other things if you did.

—JAMES BALDWIN, *NOBODY KNOWS MY NAME*

UNWITTING DOUBLE MEANINGS

Some famous words that, written in innocence, take on an unexpected sexual meaning.

*M*iss Goddard was the mistress of a ⸺ ⸺ot of
a seminary or an establishment or any
fessed, in long sentences of refined r
bine liberal acquirements with eleg
new principles and new systems, and
for enormous pay might be screw
into vanity.

⸺

*T*he coarse jollity of the
longed till the revelers were
—MACAUL

*A*nd season after seaso
spell in England, did my
in-law Charlie Hunter r
—

*A*fter three days men grow weary of a wench, a guest, and weather rainy.
—BENJAMIN FRANKLIN, *POOR RICHARD'S ALMANAC*

*H*owever weak and slender be the string
Bait it with cunt, and it will hold a king.
—ANONYMOUS, CIRCA 1700

A stiff prick has no conscience.

—FOLK SAYING

*I*f you cannot be chaste, be cautious.

—SPANISH PROVERB

A woman's "no" is said with one mouth only.

—FOLK SAYING

*W*omen are like rattlesnakes—the last thing that dies is their tail.

—OLD TEXAS SAYING

*W*hen a rogue kisses you, count your teeth.
—HEBREW PROVERB

*T*he only chaste woman is the one who has not been asked.
—SPANISH PROVERB

*W*earing a condom is like shaking hands with gloves on.
—FOLK SAYING

When the prick stands up, the brain goes to sleep.
—YIDDISH PROVERB

If it is not erotic, it is not interesting.
—FERNANDO ARRABAL

Filth and old age, I'm sure you will agree,
Are powerful wardens upon chastity.
—CHAUCER, *WIFE OF BATH'S TALE*

Just as old habits die hard, old hards die habits.
—KENNETH TYNAN

The ability to make love frivolously is the chief characteristic which distinguishes human beings from the beasts.

—HEYWOOD BROUN

What they like to give, they love to be robbed of.
—OVID, *THE ART OF LOVE*

*W*hether a pretty woman grants or withholds her favors, she always likes to be asked for them.
— OVID, *THE ART OF LOVE*

---

*G*ive me chastity and continence. But not just now.
— ST. AUGUSTINE, *CONFESSIONS*

---

*Y*ou cannot pick roses without fear of thorns, nor enjoy a fair wife without danger of horns.
— BENJAMIN FRANKLIN

She that paints her Face, thinks of her Tail.
>—BENJAMIN FRANKLIN

One should try everything once, except incest and folk dancing.
>—SIR ARNOLD BAX

As long as a person does not give up sex, sex does not give up a person.
>—GABRIEL GARCÍA MÁRQUEZ

The only known aphrodisiac is variety.
>—MARC CONNOLLY

There goes a saying, and 'twas shrewdly said,
Old fish at table, but young flesh in bed.
>—ALEXANDER POPE

The human comedy begins with a vertical smile.
>—RICHARD CONDON

I always esteemed Drunkenness the most odious of Vices. There is something to be said for Whoring: Whoring is according to nature.

—JOHN DENNIS, *THE IMPERIAL CRITIC*

*P*ornography is in the groin of the beholder.

—CHARLES REMBAR, *THE END OF OBSCENITY*

*S*ometimes a cigar is just a cigar.

—SIGMUND FREUD, ON PHALLIC DREAM SYMBOLISM

*O*h, what a tangled web we weave when first we practice to conceive.

—DON HEROLD

*W*ere kisses all the joys in bed,
One woman would another wed.
—SHAKESPEARE, *THE PASSIONATE PILGRIM*

*B*etter to sit up all night, than to go to bed with a dragon.

—JEREMY TAYLOR

"*B*ed," as the Italian proverb succinctly puts it, "is the poor man's opera."
—ALDOUS HUXLEY, *HEAVEN AND HELL*

*C*hastity is not chastity in an old man, but a disability to be unchaste.

—JOHN DONNE, *SERMONS*

A kiss can be a comma, a question mark, or an exclamation point. That's basic spelling that every woman ought to know.

—MISTINGUETT

A woman's chastity consists, like an onion, of a series of coats.

—NATHANIEL HAWTHORNE, *JOURNALS*

XI. ACTUALLY ANTI-SEX
". . . featherless bipeds in desperate congress."

Nothing in our culture, not even home computers, is more overrated than the epidermal felicity of two featherless bipeds in desperate congress.

—QUENTIN CRISP

No Sex Please—We're British
    —TITLE OF LONG-RUNNING LONDON FARCE

Sex in France is a comedy; in England it is a tragedy; in America it's a melodrama; in Italy it's an opera; in Germany, a reason to take up philosophy.

—ANONYMOUS

I am happy now that Charles calls on my bedchamber less frequently than of old. As it is, I now endure but two calls a week and when I hear his steps outside my door I lie down on my bed, close my eyes, open my legs and think of England.

—ALICE, LADY HILLINGDON, WIFE OF SECOND BARON HILLINGDON

We have no right to boast of despising and combating carnal pleasure, if we cannot feel it, if we know nothing of it, of its charms and power, and its most alluring beauties. I know both, and so have a right to speak.

—MONTAIGNE

*A*n irresistable attraction and an overwhelming repugnance and disgust.

—GEORGE BERNARD SHAW

*B*ernard Shaw was the first man to cut a swathe through the theatre and leave it strewn with virgins.

—FRANK HARRIS

*A*n old friend and mentor, Sir Clifford Norton, told me about sex education in Rugby before the First World War. The headmaster, who must have been an enlightened man, summoned all the boys who had reached the age of puberty to his study and, after reassuring himself that the door was firmly secured, made the following brief announcement: "If you touch it, it will fall off."

—PETER USTINOV, *DEAR ME*

*T*he next time you feel the desire coming on, don't give way to it. If you have the chance, just wash your parts in cold water and cool them down.

—SIR ROBERT BADEN-POWELL,
ADVICE TO BOY SCOUTS

*M*r. Mercaptan went on to preach a brilliant sermon on that melancholy sexual perversion known as continence.

—ALDOUS HUXLEY, *ANTIC HAY*

A man marries to have a home, but also because he doesn't want to be bothered with sex and all that sort of thing.

—W. SOMERSET MAUGHAM

. . . a moral vulture which steals upon our youth, silently striking its terrible talons into their vitals, and forcibly bearing them away on hideous wings to shame and death.

—ANTHONY COMSTOCK, ON EROTIC LITERATURE

*I*n males, one of the most general causes of sexual excitement is constipation. . . . When this condition is chronic, as in habitual constipation, the unnatural excitement often leads to serious results.

—DR. J. H. KELLOG, 1879

*I*ntercourse is the pure, sterile, formal expression of men's contempt for women.

—ANDREA DWORKIN

*T*he man takes a body that is not his, claims it, sows his so-called seed, reaps a harvest—he colonizes a female body, robs it of its natural resources, controls it.

—ANDREA DWORKIN

---

*I*ntercourse is an assertion of mastery, one that announces his own higher case and proves it upon a victim who is expected to surrender, serve, and be satisfied.

—KATE MILLETT

---

*S*omeone asked Sophocles, "How do you feel now about sex? Are you still able to have a woman?" He replied, "Hush, man; most glad indeed I am to be rid of it all, as though I had escaped from a mad and savage master."

—PLATO, *THE REPUBLIC*

I know it does make people happy but to me it's just like having a cup of tea.

—CYNTHIA PAYNE

---

*A*ll this fuss about sleeping together. For physical pleasure I'd sooner go to my dentist any day.

—EVELYN WAUGH

. . . a trick to perpetuate the species.
— JERRY DASHKIN

---

*I*t is certainly very hard to write about sex in English without making it sound unattractive. *Come* is a horrible word to apply to something ecstatic.
— EDMUND WILSON, *NOTEBOOKS*

---

*T*wo minutes with Venus, two years with mercury.
— DR. J. EARLE MOORE

I could be content that we might procreate like trees, without conjunction, or that there were any way to perpetuate the world without this trivial and vulgar way of coition; it is the foolishest act a wise man commits in all his life.

—THOMAS BROWNE, *RELIGIO MEDICI*

*S*ex has become one of the most discussed subjects of modern times. The Victorians pretended it did not exist; the moderns pretend that nothing else exists.

—BISHOP FULTON J. SHEEN

*W*hy should we take advice on sex from the Pope? If he knows anything about it, he shouldn't.

—GEORGE BERNARD SHAW

*'T*is the Devil inspires this evanescent ardor, in order to divert the parties from prayer.

—MARTIN LUTHER

*W*e are now all dangerously aware that sexual intercourse is a bit of a bore. What kept the "divine woman" lark going all those long, dark centuries was not an unquenchable erection but romance.

—QUENTIN CRISP

*S*tudies in which men and women are asked to rank their pleasures in order of enjoyment show repeatedly that whereas sex is the favorite for most men, many women prefer knitting.

—DR. GLENN WILSON, *THE GREAT SEX DIVIDE*

*L*ove is two minutes, fifty-two seconds of squishing noises. It shows your mind isn't clicking right.

—JOHNNY ROTTEN

*A*fter being alive, the next hardest work is sex. . . . Some people *get* energy from sex, and some people *lose* energy from sex. I have found that it's too much work. But if you have the time for it, and if you need the exercise—then you should do it.

—ANDY WARHOL

A deadly dull day. To have to make love without feeling a particle is sad work, and sad and serious did I find it.

—HENRY EDWARD FOX

*T*he act of procreation and the members employed therein are so repulsive, that if it were not for the beauty of the faces and the adornments of the actors and the pent-up impulse, nature would lose the human species.

—LEONARDO DA VINCI

*C*oition, sometimes called "the little death," is more like a slight attack of apoplexy.

—PAULINE SHAPLER, *THE FEMINIST GUIDE*

*M*y reaction to porno films is as follows: After the first ten minutes, I want to go home and screw. After the first twenty minutes, I never want to screw again as long as I live.

—ERICA JONG

*I*mpotence and sodomy are socially O.K., but birth control is flagrantly middle class.
—EVELYN WAUGH, JOKINGLY TO NANCY MITFORD

*F*ully one half of all women seldom or never experience any pleasure whatever in the sexual act. Now this is an impeachment of nature, a disgrace to our civilization.
—VICTORIA WOODHULL

A love affair nowadays is a tableau of two wild animals, each with its teeth sunk in the other's neck, each scared to let go in case it bleeds to death.
—KENNETH TYNAN

*M*y editor told me that the second half of the book needed a damn good love scene, and there is nothing I dislike writing more. Love-making is such a nonverbal

thing. I hate that explicit "he stuck it in her" kind of thing because it is so boring. You can only say "he stuck it in her" so many ways.
—COLLEEN MCCULLOUGH, IN AN INTERVIEW CONCERNING HER NOVEL, *THE THORN BIRDS*

*I*t would be a a sad thing indeed if love were limited to the mere act which grocers and their mates perform at midnight in the middle of a four poster. We are not the lower animals, Hilda . . . .
—GEORGE MOORE, LETTER TO HILDA HAWTHORNE

*L*ove between the sexes is a sin in theology, a forbidden intercourse in jurisprudence, a mechanical insult in medicine, and a subject philosophy has no time for.
—KARL KRAUS

XII. SOME DEFINITIONS OF SEX
"Whoever called it necking . . ."

*W*hoever called it necking was a poor judge of anatomy.
—GROUCHO MARX

---

*S*ome things are better than sex, and some are worse, but there's nothing exactly like it.
—W. C. FIELDS

---

*T*his is the game of twenty toes,
It's played all over town;
The girls they play with ten toes up,
The boys with ten toes down.
—ENGLISH FOLK RHYME

. . .[*S*omething] popular because it's centrally located.
—SHANNON CARSE

---

*S*ex touches the heavens only when it simultaneously touches the gutter and the mud.
—GEORGE JEAN NATHAN

*T*he formula by which one and one makes three.
—LEONARD L. LEVINSON

———— • • ————

*S*ex is the great amateur art. The professional, male or female, is frowned on; he or she misses the whole point and spoils the show.
—DAVID CORT, *SOCIAL ASTONISHMENTS*

———— • • ————

. . . I think sex is a part of everything. I don't think of sex as just something that happens now and then. I

can't imagine writing without the feel of sex. I mean sex is a diffuse feeling. It diffuses everything and only once in a while would it be called sex.

—NELSON ALGREN

A perfectly normal, almost commonplace activity . . . of the same nature as dancing or tennis.

—ALDOUS HUXLEY

*I*n America sex is an obsession, in other parts of the world it is a fact.

—MARLENE DIETRICH

*B*usiness is like sex; when it's good, it's very, very good; when it's not so good, it's still good.

—MERVYN A. KING, LONDON SCHOOL OF ECONOMICS

*F*inding the cool satisfaction of heaven in the heated embers of the pit . . . .

—WARREN GOLDBERG

*S*ex is when the loin lies down with the limb.
—CONRAD AIKEN

———— • •————

Give sex the the respect it deserves. There are those, I will name no names, who have been trying to take sex out of the realm of the frivolous and put it into the realm of the trivial. The discoverers of the G-spot, for example. Those who go to singles bars and pick up men wearing medallions who they don't even like. Those who think romance is dead. Romance is not dead! Sex is important! Sex is profound! Sex is funny!
—CYNTHIA HEIMEL,
SEX TIPS FOR GIRLS

———— • •————

*T*he last important human activity not subject to tax-ation . . . .
—RUSSELL BAKER

———— • •————

A clever imitation of love. It has all the action but none of the plot.
—WILLIAM ROTSLER

*A*t 60 . . . the sexual preoccupation, when it hits you, seems sometimes sharper, as if it were an elderly malady, like gout.

—EDMUND WILSON

*W*hat is lust, adult lust, after all, but the desire to recapture the heady sensations of adolescent sexuality?
—WILLIAM BOYD, *THE NEW CONFESSIONS*

*A*ll this talk about sex, all this worry about sex—big deal. The sun makes me happy. I eat a good fish, he makes me happy. I sleep with a good man, he makes me happy.

—MELINA MERCOURI

*T*he thing that takes up the least amount of time and causes the most amount of trouble . . . .

—JOHN BARRYMORE

*T*he Tabasco sauce which an adolescent national palate sprinkles on every course in the menu . . . .

—MARY D. WINN

*S*ex appeal is 50 percent what you've got and 50 percent what people think you've got.

—SOPHIA LOREN

*E*rotic love is the spindle on which the earth turns.

—OCTAVIO PAZ

*F*reud found sex an outcast in the outhouse, and left it in the living room an honored guest.
—W. BERTRAM WOLFE

*S*omething the children never discuss in the presence of their elders . . . .
—ARTHUR S. ROCHE

*T*he poor man's polo . . . .
—CLIFFORD ODETS